MANAGING
INFORMATION
OVERLOAD

The WorkSmart Series

MANAGING INFORMATION OVERLOAD

Lynn Lively

amacom

AMERICAN MANAGEMENT ASSOCIATION

THE WORKSMART SERIES

New York • Atlanta • Boston • Chicago • Kansas City • San Francisco • Washington, D.C.
Brussels • Toronto • Mexico City

This book is available at a special
discount when ordered in bulk quantities.
For information, contact Special Sales Department,
AMACOM, a division of American Management Association,
1601 Broadway, New York, NY 10019.

This publication is designed to provide accurate and authoritative information in regard to the subject matter covered. It is sold with the understanding that the publisher is not engaged in rendering legal, accounting, or other professional service. If legal advice or other expert assistance is required, the services of a competent professional person should be sought.

Library of Congress Cataloging-in-Publication Data

Lively, Lynn.
    Managing information overload / Lynn Lively.
        p.   cm — (The WorkSmart series)
    ISBN 0-8144-7842-5
    1. Personal information management.   2. Information resources management.   3. Information technology—Management.   I. Title.
II. Series.
HD69.T54L588   1996
650.1—dc20   96-18552
                                              CIP

Printing number

10   9   8   7   6   5   4   3   2   1

CONTENTS

PREFACE

You can't know it all.

Let me repeat: As a human being with limited time, money, and energy, you will never know everything you want to, should, or would like to.

You can, however, know everything you *need* to know. You can feel confident that you are speaking with the authority that comes from solid, inarguable data. You can find things quickly, and stop feeling so overloaded and poorly organized. You can become a master of interpreting the subtle and hearing the unspoken, so you spot trends before they are public knowledge. In short, you can control information, tap its power, and benefit from its wealth of potential.

This book shows you how to get that desk cleaned off, new journals read, reports reviewed, rumors researched, and your computer's hard drive better organized. It will also show you how to get maximum benefit out of all the information that's available to you. The secret is to manage information just as you would manage any other important resource. You have to make it work for you, not the other way around!

Information is the driver of every decision you make, and decisions constitute the process by which you create your career and life. Use good information, and you make wise decisions that lead you along the path of success. Quote unreliable info that wrecks your credibility, or miss an important requirement buried in fine print such that your application is rejected, or fail to learn about a trend that is shaping your industry, and you will find your career going downhill. There is no better long-term investment you can make in yourself than to improve your information management skills and techniques.

Conquering information overload is a two-part process. Part I of this book shows you a new and powerful way of looking at information. You learn how to decide what you need to know by identifying and organizing the key information that is important to you. This key information is a reflection of the important parts of your professional life; it is where you will focus your information management efforts.

Next you use the tips, techniques, and suggestions in Part II to more efficiently and effectively mangage incoming and outgoing information, whether it be personal conversations, e-mail, reports and printouts, or junk mail.

Once you know what is important and are in control, you are ready to harness the power of the information flow to shape your future. You'll read smarter, question better, and find good sources. You'll use information to form your own opinions and think for yourself so that you become a respected leader of projects, committees, teams, task forces, departments, and ultimately your own destiny.

Information overload is increasing. The people who are tomorrow's success stories (and your competition) know waiting won't help; they are mastering those piles of information now. They're the ones eager for the unexpected and for the opportunity new information brings. Be one of them!

This book was written to help you work smart at your desk, on the phone, and in your meetings. My wish for you is an interesting—which is not the same as easy—journey along the path to becoming an Information Master. Turn the page and let's get started—*today.*

PART

MANAGING YOURSELF

What do you need to know?

Never let anyone else answer this question for you.

How could another person possibly know the details of your job as well as you? After all, you are the only person who spends eight hours per day doing what you do. How could your boss know the ins and outs of the reports you prepare? The meetings you coordinate? The customer service you provide? Even if he or she used to have your job, things change.

Bosses, coworkers, and other people can certainly help, offer suggestions, and give direction. But you and you alone hold final responsibility for deciding what you need to know to be a standout in your job.

The first step in overcoming information overload is to manage yourself. You do that by deciding what you need to know. Whether you're a production supervisor, executive assistant, small-business owner, marketing professional, account exec, safety manager, or credit processor, by using the techniques in Part I you will find the confidence it takes to become an Information Master.

CHAPTER 1

Getting Organized:
The Reverse Approach

You've started reading this book because *today is the day:* the day you are going to get organized.

Why today? Perhaps you are grimly determined not to be embarrassed when your boss walks into your office and again comments on "the earthquake that must have hit." Maybe you've just gotten a promotion, inherited a new office, and it needs to be organized. Or you vow people will not have to call you at home the next time you are sick because they can't find the budget summaries. Whatever the reason, becoming an Information Master has risen to the top of your to-do list.

YOU ARE IN INFORMATION OVERLOAD WHEN:

- You miss an important deadline and angrily protest you were never told. Later you find the due date on the second page of the transmittal summary you haven't read yet.
- With despair, you realize all those great ideas you got at your last conference are gathering dust in a notebook on your credenza.
- You lie awake nights worrying where a confidential folder you were compiling on a poorly performing employee could possibly have gotten to.
- You feel your face flame when your boss asks you, for the third time, where the latest sum-

> mary is that was supposed to be on her desk last Monday.
> - You lose a promotion to a coworker who volunteered for a new assignment because he ''was caught up and eager for new opportunities.''
> - You realize you are totally dependent on a technician to transmit your computer files because you haven't learned the upgraded system yet.
> - You fear that your value to your department is lessening because your industry knowledge is getting out of date, and you can't imagine how you can cram in any more reading.

INFORMATION DEFINED

The first step in overcoming information overload is to . . . create new file folders? Get out the wastebasket? Order a bookcase? Wrong. Wrong. And wrong again. The first step is to do nothing. Do nothing, that is, but keep reading. Yes, that's right; don't touch those piles—yet.

It's time to rethink your approach. Let's face it, information overload is increasing. Computers are generating ever more reports, e-mail is adding more and more messages, and meetings are on the increase. Instead of striving for the appearance of neatness that only lasts until the next time you leave your office for a few days of vacation or a business trip, it's time for a new strategy. One that goes beyond cosmetics, one that will solve your problem for the rest of your professional career, one that is not just a temporary fix.

THE NATURE OF INFORMATION

Information is knowledge expressed in any form.

Lean back and pause. Think what that statement means. First it means that the knowledge base, like the world, is

What Is Information?

Information is knowledge expressed in any form. It includes but is not limited to:

* Hard copy: things you can hold such as books, journals, reports, mail, and faxes
* Verbal: phone calls, conversations, and gossip
* Electronic: e-mail, the Internet, and what is on videotapes, computer hard drives, and floppy disks

But it's more. Information includes:

* A novel or movie that changes forever the way you perceive Wall Street, or equal opportunity
* Observation of a lingering touch between two coworkers that suggests they are having an affair
* The sinking realization that a breakthrough technology is going to make your product line obsolete

In short, information reflects life in all its marvelous complexity.

enormous. What that translates to is that not you, not your boss, not the president, nobody can know it all. So give up that fantasy right now.

Information is also neutral. It's not good or bad, right or wrong, helpful or harmful. It just is, that's all. How it is interpreted and used is up to you. Read about any courtroom discussion and you'll see even "truth" is not self-evident.

If you can't know it all, what can you know? What should you know? That's what you're going to find out next.

IDEAL INFORMATION

Ideal information is:

- Current: not out-of-date, the latest version available, timely.
- Sufficient: enough to do your job well. (Forget "complete." There's no such thing, and even if there were you don't have the time or money it would take to get complete information.)
- Essential: what you must have to perform your job and make your decisions. ("Nice to have" information? Few companies can afford that anymore.)
- Reliable: accurate, trustworthy.
- Verifiable: reproducible, what other prudent people doing the same thing you did would come up with.

Are there exceptions to these guidelines? Sure, but keeping them in mind will help you determine what is ideal information *for you*. Then you can make wise exceptions, and defend them. "Yes, I know this is last week's report, but the numbers for this department didn't change and that's the only part I used."

INFORMATION MASTERS

You haven't touched anything yet, have you? Good. Because now you're ready to get organized. Following the system in this book will turn you into an information master—provided, of course, that this book doesn't end up in a stack gathering dust like all those other books you haven't read yet. (Just kidding, but please, at least keep mine on top!)

Information masters have created a system for balancing the flow of incoming and outgoing information that works for them. They know how to create, use, and dispose of information; have realistic expectations about the strengths and limits of information; and use information as a primary decision-making resource to supplement the power of their minds. They know the information they use is a reflection of what is important to them.

Your goal is to become an information master:

- You convince others because your facts are more relevant than their facts.
- You get promotions because your work is done on time, within budget, and without dumping unfairly on other people.
- You rarely get behind or overwhelmed to the point of despair.
- You make sound decisions that keep customers happy and the company profitable.

Notice we haven't talked about facts, statistics, or data yet. Those are forms of *expression* of information. You want to go deeper than that. You want to decide what you need to know.

To do that, you're going to use the reverse approach. When overwhelmed by information, most people first attempt to neaten up their desks. Although your workspace may then look (temporarily) tidy, the tidiness almost never lasts. The reason is that your *thinking* and your *need* for information aren't yet organized.

THE REVERSE APPROACH

You're going to use a better approach. First you're going to neaten up your mind. Then do your office a bit later. (Incidentally, throughout this book you'll see the words *office, workspace, desk,* and *cubicle*. They all mean the same thing: the area where you use information to do your job.)

The first steps are so easy you won't believe it. Information, like anything else, is mastered small step by small step. Let's start now. (I'm assuming that (1) you're at work and (2) you can get up right now, either to get away or to find a quiet and solitary place at work for one hour.)

Step A: Get out your briefcase . . . or a plastic bag.

Step B: Put as many of the following items into it as you have readily available. (Don't have very many? Just do the best you can and don't let that be an excuse to quit or procrastinate.) First, gather your planning tools:

- This book
- Your current job description
- Your most recent performance evaluation
- Your current calendar
- Your planning notebooks
- Your work schedules
- Your to-do lists
- Similar documents for last year and/or next year
- Written statements of personal and professional values, goals, and/or mission statements, and any related documents you might have prepared

Now gather up your supplies, too:

- Highlighter
- Pencil and pen
- Scrap paper, for example, old computer printouts with one side blank
- Six manila folders
- A clipboard to write on
- Lined notebook or yellow legal paper
- Tape
- Scissors

Leave your laptop computer, pager, and cellular phone in the office for now. (Oh, come on, you can risk being out of touch just this once!) Take a chance. Just do it. Overcoming information overload is worth your full attention.

Caution number one: *Do not take any original documents out of the office without permission.* Use good judgment. Can you make a photocopy? Find an extra set of documents? If absolutely not, can you get permission to work in an empty conference room in your building?

Caution number two: *Do not take confidential, financial, or otherwise sensitive materials out of the office without permission.* Check with your boss first.

Good, you have gathered up as much as you can and you've pried yourself loose. What's next?

Step C: Leave your desk, cubicle, or office, with your plastic bag or briefcase in hand. Walk away from the clutter, piles, and unanswered phone messages. If you're not leaving the building, there's no need to walk far. Just far enough to find a place where you can sit by yourself and be uninterrupted for one hour. Maybe you'll need to come in early, extend your lunch hour, or negotiate with your boss for extra time. But somehow you've got to get away for sixty minutes so you can perform Step D.

Step D: Sit alone at a table and arrange your planning tools in a semicircle about two feet in front of you. Put the scrap paper directly in front of you, ready to write on. Pick up a pencil.

Congratulations, you've taken the first steps. And they are the hardest. Breathe deeply! You're no longer just moaning and worrying; you've begun.

You are ready to decide what information is important to you, and what isn't. Chapter 2 shows you how. But don't even skip ahead until you've actually carried out these four steps, until you've gathered your planning tools and supplies, are alone, and are ready to concentrate. With all the work you've got to do, you want to do this once and do it right.

THINK PUZZLE, NOT STRUGGLE

Imagine yourself winding your way through a complicated maze with many twists and turns, false starts, and dead ends. The process of finding a route is one of discovery. It takes time, but it's interesting and fun. Ultimately you emerge on the other side, triumphantly having found your own path.

That's just what you're going to do here. Overcoming information overload is also a process. You're looking for "a way," not "The Way," to become an Information Master. And given how interested you are in shaping your own process, it's going to be fun.

CHAPTER 2

SOLVING A PUZZLE: WHAT'S IMPORTANT TO YOU?

If you can't know it all, what can you know?

You can know everything that is *important to you*—once you figure out what that is. You reach that point (in this chapter) by systematically identifying five areas of expertise you are committed to mastering. Once they are identified, five corresponding areas of information will become apparent. Then you'll be ready to return to your workplace and follow the suggestions in Chapter 3 on how to attack the piles on your desk.

Ready? Set? Let's go—away from your workspace, remember? With all your tools and supplies spread out at a table in front of you. First read through the following steps. Feel free to turn to the completed examples at the end of this chapter at any time. After reading these steps, just start writing. Do the easiest part first.

THE INFORMATION IDENTIFICATION PROCESS

The following exercise will provide focus:

> Step 1. Decide what you think is important.
> Step 2. Reconcile that with what your company thinks is important.
> Step 3. List the information needed to do what is important.
> Step 4. Resolve questions.

STEPS TO INFORMATION IDENTIFICATION

Step 1. Decide What You Think Is Important

This is an interesting process. By following the steps provided, you mentally test your assumptions before you move anything in your office. That way you'll have fewer areas to rework later.

First, design your worksheets. Put your name and today's date on the top of three sheets of paper. Label each sheet across the top:

First draft 1, "Job parts," focuses on the most important areas, parts, duties, and responsibilities of your job.

First draft 2, "Self-improvement," asks what you are not very good at and need/want to improve.

First Draft 1: Job Parts

The most important areas, parts, duties, and responsibilities of my job.

First Draft 2: Self-Improvement

What I am not very good at and need/want to improve.

First Draft 3: Future Development

New technologies, knowledge, and skills that will be important to my career success twelve to twenty-four months from now.

First draft 3, "Future development," covers new technologies, knowledge, and skills that will be important to your career success twelve to twenty-four months from now.

Next, fill in each page of your first drafts. To complete first draft 1, try to think of ten different things you are paid to do. (Use a pencil so your mind knows you won't be doing this perfectly the first time.)

Note: If you have already set clear goals, good for you; this part will be easy. If you are new at this it will take longer, and you might want to consider getting some training in goal setting.

Tip: This is only a first draft; just write.

Remember: you are preparing a first draft. By definition, it is impossible for you to make a mistake or be wrong! Put down anything you want to, no matter how ridiculous. Your heart speaks first; your head will come in soon enough. Just write for fifteen minutes.

Now complete first draft 2, "Self-improvement." Nobody is perfect: what are you not very good at? Be honest with yourself. Absolutely no one will see these entries unless you want them to.

Complete first draft 3, "Future development." These are new areas you intend to pursue. Let yourself dream a little. Ask yourself, "To get a promotion, I'll need to be good at ———." Or perhaps say to yourself, "Gee, it would be fun to work on ———."

Step 2. Reconcile With What Your Company Thinks Is Important

Now, item by item, read or just skim the planning tools you have brought with you. Compare them to what you have written on each of your three first drafts. You are looking for confirmation that what you think is important matches what your job description, your bosses, and your work plans say is important.

Now use your highlighter to flag inconsistencies between your first drafts and your job description, work plan, etc.

Tip: Cut and paste.

On an extra sheet, note any questions to ask your boss, things that need to be updated on your job description or business plan, etc.

Idea: Use your scissors to cut up your first draft so that you have one idea or thought per piece of paper. Then move the scraps around as if they were playing cards. Mix and match ideas. Tape the pieces together to form a new draft. Expensive consultants get paid lots of money to do fun things like this!

Prepare revised sheets using fresh paper. Narrow down the most important parts of your job to three areas; use one sheet for each. Next, narrow your self-improvement and future development areas to one sheet each. Combine, cut out, prioritize, and do whatever is necessary to pare your lists in the self-improvement and future development areas to a few sentences. Look at the samples at the end of this chapter for inspiration.

Label these five resulting worksheets Job Part 1, Job Part 2, Job Part 3, Self-improvement, and Future Development. Recopy as necessary. (That's why you brought all the scrap paper.) Crunch up and throw away all those drafts as your thinking progresses.

Note: Sure, you can have just one job part sheet. But if you look closely, your job probably has several parts. Break it up the best you can.

Sure, you could also have ten job part sheets. But aren't you setting yourself up to sink again? Remember, you can't know it all. You need to choose where to focus.

On yet another sheet of paper write down or recopy:

> Questions to ask your boss
> Information you are missing
> People to call
> Any other good ideas you have had during this drafting

Combine your remaining items, questions, and miscellaneous highlighted items on this follow-up page. Take a minute

Tip: Your lists should not overwhelm or discourage you; they're meant to *help* you.

to congratulate yourself on how your thinking is progressing.

Step 3. List the Information Needed to Do What Is Important

Now you're ready to think about the information you need to do your job, improve yourself, and grow. On each sheet draw a line below your writing. Now start listing the information that is required to *complete* each area of upcoming activity. Draw another line across the lower third of the page and beneath it list any miscellaneous questions, thoughts, and ideas. Notice the sample sheets at the end of the chapter (Figures 2-1, 2-2, and 2-3), which have been included to inspire you.

WHAT *NOT* TO DO:

Here are a few traps that you don't want to fall into:

1. Make your lists as concrete as possible. For example, don't say you are going to "file every piece of paper the day it comes in." Instead, put down "file the weekly customer service summaries each Friday."
2. Put down what's important to you to get your job done or develop yourself. Don't write what you "should" say. Also, just because your boss doesn't care if you improve your computer skills doesn't mean that you can't pursue it. You're the one responsible for yourself and your future.
3. Use positive, professional language. For example, perhaps spreadsheets have you confused and you hate them. But you realize they are an absolutely critical part of your work. Remind yourself that spreadsheets are information;

> information is neutral; and you can learn to be a "spreadsheet master" if it means you will advance. Force yourself to use positive—or at least neutral—language and an eager tone. You, not the spreadsheet, are the area of improvement.

Step 4. Resolve Questions

Take your six manila folders, and put one sheet in each folder, along with anything else that is relevant to that key area. Label the folders Job Part 1, etc., in pencil. Put your questions and miscellaneous stuff in folder six; label it Information Master: Misc. Throw away earlier drafts, so they won't confuse you later. Make sure everything is dated.

Return to your office, workspace, or shop. Do not touch any of those stacks yet! Remember, you are only going to handle them once and handle them right, and you're not quite ready.

Tip: Separate boss problems from information problems.

Instead, make an appointment with your boss to go over your three job-part sheets. It is very important to get agreement that there is a match between what you think is most important and what your boss thinks is most important. What you are doing is committing yourself to stay on top of those areas at all costs and not to let them slip.

If you and your boss can't agree on what's important, you don't have an information problem; you have a boss problem that needs to be solved first.

You may want to meet with more than your boss. If you're on a team, perhaps you will want to run the relevant job-part sheet by the team leader. Or your executive assistant, staff, etc. It's up to you. Just be sure you are truly seeking input, not procrastinating.

Don't have a boss? Run it by your board of advisors, trusted peers, or key staff people. Broaden your perspective. Look for someone who sees the world a bit differently than you do.

Question: Should you show your boss your self-improvement and future development sheets? *Answer:* That's up to you, but why not? Your boss is probably just as painfully aware as you are of what you're not very good at and would love to see signs of improvement. And he or she is not a mind reader. How can your boss know where you'd like to grow if you don't say so?

Now if you wish, you are ready to prepare nice labels for the five folders holding your revised draft pages and a clean copy of each page. You can even enter them into your computer. But it's not necessary. The sheets will probably be refined some more as you begin to work with them. If you can stand it, let things stay messy for a while so you're not annoyed when they have to be changed.

Congratulations. You are ready to go on to Chapter 3 and finally start cleaning up that mess at work. But first, how about a break? You've earned a nice cup of herbal tea! You're on your way to becoming an information master.

Figure 2-1.   Sample job sheet for Joyce Terry.

Job Sheet #1:   *Joyce Terry, Date: _____*

As a safety professional my most important job duty is to keep all the ~~OSHA~~ Federal, state, county, and city regulations updated and available for reference.

Information Needed:
> **All incoming regulations from government agencies*
> **Master notebooks with tabs*
> **Safety council journals and publications*
> **Legal references*

*Missing Information: Current regulations for Washington State to cover new plant opening there.

Miscellaneous:
> *Who keeps workers comp guidelines — me or Human Resources?*
> *Question: How long do superseded pages need to be kept? Old copies dating back to 1991 are in my office.*
> *Idea: Could any of this info be kept in law library? They have more space!*

Figure 2-2. Sample job sheet for Jim Nathan.

Future Development *Jim Nathan, Date:* _____

To grow my repair business, I need to know how to upgrade our test equipment as new models come out.

Information Needed:

   — complete schematics and Owners Manuals

   — List of all test equipment *★and upgrades* *listed on inventory records*

   — Catalogs of newest product models

Ideas:

   ? Check out vocational schools and see how they do this.
   ? Would Chris like to help with this project?

Figure 2–3. Sample job sheet for Kurt Sang.

Self-Improvement Sheet.   *Kurt Sang, Date:_____*

I would like to contribute more in staff meetings because my ideas are good and other people often come up with them several months later. Speaking up would help me get promoted. But I am shy and my family has taught me to be polite.

Information Needed:
  — Schedule of assertiveness classes
  — ESL tapes so I can practice

Ideas:
  Can I help boss prepare agenda for staff meetings so I can get extra time to prepare my ideas?
  I could volunteer to help.

CHAPTER 3

DIGGING OUT IMPORTANT INFORMATION

You're now at your cubicle, workstation, or office and ready to begin. You're clear on what five areas of information you are going to master. Your boss has agreed. You have a half hour or more to make progress. At last it's time to start organizing. But don't pick up any stacks yet! Instead . . .

SCAN YOUR WORKSPACE

Sit in your chair and do a slow scan of your workspace. Turn a full 360 degrees. Ignore all the paper, books, and things lying around and in the file cabinets. Instead, let yourself see only work spaces, such as desk, file cabinet, bookcase, etc. Notice your equipment: computer, printer, phone, calculator. Pretend you have a new office.

Now, in your mind think about your three top job parts and the information they require. Picture yourself actually performing those three most important tasks. Notice how you use the information each part requires. Fill in the blanks with a Yes/No or note to yourself. Do you:

☐ Look things up in reference manuals?
☐ Write lots of letters on your computer?
☐ Update your database while telephoning customers?
☐ Make handwritten notes while on the phone with colleagues?

21

☐ Spread out lots of material on a table for report preparation?

☐ Sketch and draft for layouts?

Add other tasks that you do.

CREATE A WORK FLOW SHEET

Get out a piece of paper and create a work flow sheet, with four columns. The ideas listed above are a starting point to help you think through your work locations for your three job focus areas. Add your own observations to your list. Do the sheets for your self-improvement and future development areas.

Figure 3-1 is an example of a work flow sheet.

Tip: Not all information is in your office.

Take a minute again, to think of other key sources of information that are not here in your workspace. Examples might be central files, the library, or another department. If it's not feasible to have copies yourself of all the information that's not here, create reminder sheets so you won't forget to refer to the missing sources. For example, "Remember to review insurance policies stored in fireproof file cabinets."

Take your work flow sheet and write down where the information should be located to make your three most important job duties easy. You're missing a piece of furniture such as a shelf or book rack? Make a note of it.

Figure 3-1. Sample work flow sheet.

Job Task:	Info Needed:	Work Location:	Ideal Info Location:
1. Maintain database	1. Sales lead forms	1. Computer keyboard	1. Shelf above monitor
2. Production scheduling	2. Weekly inventory and sales orders	2. Table	2. Propped upright on my table
3. Sign off weekly reports	3. Current drafts and history files	3. Desktop	3. Top two file drawers

Sit in your chair and slowly turn in another complete circle. Expand your field of focus a bit further out, to your walls, windows, and dividers. Notice whether your calendar is easy to see. Are your awards on display, to provide positive reinforcement? Is your pencil sharpener handy? Are your shelves stable for the weight they carry?

Notice what works with the way your workspace is now arranged and what doesn't. Make notes of what you want to move, replace, or get rid of.

For the moment, ignore all the information that doesn't relate to your three most important job duties. (We deal with the excess in Chapter 4.)

PICK AN APPROACH

Now comes what you have been waiting for ever since you started this book. Congratulations for being so disciplined. This is the fun part, where you actually move things around and see results. However, be forewarned: Things will look messier before they look better. It's like taking your house apart for a thorough cleaning: All the pieces are scattered and only at the end do they come together to look neat and tidy.

Five Possible Approaches

There are five different ways to rearrange your workspace to fit your work flow sheets:

1. Organize one shelf or surface area at time.
2. Clean up one pile or stack of material at a time.
3. Assemble one major project or assignment at a time.
4. Leave existing things the way they are and begin with new information as it flows into your office.
5. Take apart your entire workspace and do everything at once.

Tip: Group information by content, not form.

Grouping information by content, not form, means that all books, reports, journals, and tapes that relate to one of your major job tasks are placed together. The appearance or form that the information takes (what you might think of as the "category" of the piece) doesn't matter. Think "project" rather than "category."

With this in mind, now look at the pluses and minuses of each of the five approaches, and pick the one that works best for you.

PERSPECTIVE: THINK YOU DON'T HAVE TIME FOR THIS PROJECT?

You're already spending the time: spending it looking for things, worrying, and missing important opportunities. Taking time to learn how to overcome information overload is not wasting time; it's investing in your future. And remember, this major reorganization won't go on forever. You'll soon have a system so you won't get bogged down again.

Physically Matching the List to Reality

Which way should you proceed? Take out your calendar and see what's coming up today, this week, for the next month, for the next year. What sort of time intervals do you see available for this project?

If your work is seasonal and you're slow around the holidays, for example, perhaps you should wait and do approach five, tackling everything at once in the week between Christmas and New Year's. *Caution:* Approach five works best for the more experienced info master who is certain how he or she needs to be organized.

If this is the first time you have looked at your information flows, keep in mind that this is a work in progress and it will be tweaked as time goes on. Even if you had the time, you probably couldn't do a one-time cleanup that would last. Start small.

If you have a major new project beginning in two weeks, that's a perfect place to begin. Create a shelf for that project. Use approach four, and go forward from where you are. Root around in your existing piles and stacks *only* to pull out work that is relevant to the new project you are beginning.

If there are no schedule breaks in sight, then select any of the first three options and begin small. Pick a pile, and start going through it item by item.

Nibbling away at your piles offers the best chance for success. For all but the self-employed or an independent contractor, getting a full week to take your workspace apart is unlikely. Typically the interruptions and external demands upon your time are unceasing. If you are able to sort through and organize one shelf or pile per week, you are making real progress. (*Idea:* Use one coffee break a week?)

As you concentrate your related information, set up catch areas. These are empty spaces where you can store items related to your job tasks as they come in so that they don't get lost. You empty them out regularly by filing, updating, or discarding superseded materials. It's where you put priority items from your in basket or things you bring into your office.

Question: Should I have one catch area, or more than one, for every new project?

Answer: One per priority area is simplest, but two would work: one for high-priority info, one for reading.

Workspace Checklist

☐ Each of your three most important job parts has one or more shelves, file cabinets, or sections where all the work is clustered.
☐ Information that you use frequently is readily accessible. For example, your software guidebooks are placed directly above or near your computer.

☐ Related information is grouped together. External appearances don't concern you; it's OK if books are in different spots in your office.

☐ Inactive or low-priority information is not taking up prime space. (What to do with it? See Chapter 4.)

☐ As much as possible, your workspace is arranged so that when you are concentrating on one of your three most important duties, you aren't distracted by seeing other areas. Your computer screen and phone face one way so you can do, say, job part 1, for example, update sales leads as you talk. Your desktop faces another direction for job part 2, preparing and editing reports. Your table is kept clear of everything but the project folders needed for job part 3, meeting with your team members.

Of course, your system isn't perfect. But important things all have a place, so you waste far less time rummaging around. You know these techniques are honing your concentration and increasing your productivity.

GOOD WORK VS. GOOD APPEARANCES

How much money should you spend getting new furniture? New file folders? Fancy printed labels? That depends on your budget and tolerance for shopping. The thing to remember is that you can overcome information overload with cardboard boxes and cast-off shelving. You may not particularly like shabby furniture and scratched out, re-used file folders. But don't confuse good appearances with good work.

If your company has formal methods and procedures, strict filing rules, etc., follow them. Otherwise you will create extra work for other people, and they will hate you. Get creative. For example, include a photocopy of the front page of an infrequently used manual on your job part shelf to remind you to go pull the original when you need to work with it. Or ask your boss if it would be possible for you to get your own set of reference manuals if you can prove you truly are wasting lots of time searching for frequently used materials.

Reminder: You are developing a system to organize your mind, not replacing or modifying the companywide organization.

THE ART OF CONTINUOUS IMPROVEMENT

Just when you finally have your space for job part 1 organized, things change. Perhaps you're now required to make plans weekly instead of monthly. Or you have to integrate a new software package into your work.

You're disheartened.

Don't be! You didn't do anything wrong. The puzzle has just gotten more interesting. Besides, you're smarter today than you were yesterday.

Future Development and Self-Improvement Sheets

You are ready to find a place for your two remaining information master areas. Look around your office again. This time you don't need prime space, or even much space—maybe just part of a file drawer, or one corner of a bookcase. Pick a spot where you can group the information related to these two projects. Leave enough room to accumulate new information. Now that you are committed to personal growth and future development, it's amazing what you'll see that relates to these two topics. Collect it all. Schedule progress time monthly.

What a relief: Your important information is under control. But what about the rest? On to Chapter 4, cleaning up the leftovers.

CHAPTER 4

CLEANING UP LEFTOVER PILES, FILES, AND STACKS

You're making progress. Your workspace doesn't look 100 percent perfect yet, but you have now concentrated the information relating to the three most important parts of your job plus your personal priorities.

But what about the rest of your workspace? What do you do with the remaining piles, stacks, books, folders, computer printouts, etc.? There is no perfect solution. But this chapter gives you options you can adapt to make them work for you.

CONFRONTING YOUR HOUSECLEANING FEARS

You knew this was coming. It's time to get rid of some stuff. You want to, but you really don't see how it can be done. Everything is soooo important. Well, Info Master To Be: It's time to confront your fears.

THE TOP TWELVE INFORMATION EXCUSES

Here's a list of reasons why you may be reluctant to part with some of those stacks in your office.

If I get rid of information:

1. I'll be missing something important.
2. Someone will yell at me.

---

3. Something terrible will happen and it will be my fault.
4. I won't be "in the know."
5. I won't look productive if my workspace isn't piled up.
6. I'll spend more time looking around for information in the future.
7. I'll lose my creativity and become some kind of neatness freak.
8. My office mate will encroach on my empty space.
9. I won't be able to look busy (even if I'm just strolling down my personal memory lane).
10. That project represents years of work; it's important to have those boxes of (pick one: surveys, inventory forms, budget drafts, etc.) around me.
11. Add your own: I have to _____.
12. Come on, get really honest and confess it all: You don't _____.

Notice that all the excuses come down to fear! Fears are real. All of the above are possible consequences of throwing something out. But are they probable? Let's examine them one at a time.

"I'll Be Missing Something Important."

You have already identified what's important with your three job parts, so it is very unlikely you'll miss something really important once you throw old things out. However, if a fourth job part keeps popping up over and over, there's no reason you can't add another area and create a home for all that information as well.

Think about what's more likely to happen. By concentrating and clearing things out, you'll be able to put your fingers more quickly on what's really important to help you shine at your job.

"Someone Will Yell at Me."

Yes, that's possible. But it's unlikely, because you are obviously good at producing everything you have responsibility for keeping. Someone is more likely to yell at you when they quickly need key information from you and you *can't* produce it accurately and quickly.

"Something Terrible Will Happen and It Will Be All My Fault."

Come now, are you really that powerful? This is a pure ego trip. First, nothing terrible is likely to happen if you get rid of those piles. But even if something did, how would it all be your fault? Are you playing some old family tapes here? You're not four years old and you didn't cause your parents' divorce!

Tip: Most information can be re-created.

Then there is the "re-creation risk," the possibility that information will have to be painfully reconstructed, for an IRS audit, for example. In dealing with this belief, you have to balance inconvenience, costs, and probabilities. This is a specialized area well beyond the scope of this book. If you want to learn more, take a class on records management at your community college.

Things that can usually be re-created include:

> Canceled checks
> Bank statements
> Tax returns
> Insurance policies
> Anything on computer disk
> Reports, as long as one copy exists somewhere
> Anything with a drawing or part number

Things that are hard to re-create:

> Original entries on a computer (*Note:* If you are not
> backing up your data frequently, BEGIN NOW.

This fear is real; you could get yelled at loudly for this one.)
Original artwork
Original notes
Original signatures
Original lists of resources and key people
Original research
Original time cards
Samples
Prototypes

Notice how the word *original* keeps coming up? That's your key word for determining which are vital records to protect.

"I Won't Be 'In the Know.' "

Now you've found a reason that has to be dealt with. Here are some thoughts.

- You will (I emphasize WILL) be in the know about what *is important* to you. You have identified areas where you will concentrate and be the expert.
- You can't be in the know about everything; it is not humanly possible. Furthermore, as you put less and less energy into lower priorities, you won't be in the know very long anyway. You'll just be wrong a lot because you'll be passing on old information.
- What a great chance to form an alliance with the person who really is in the know about this area. Offer the person all your history files and past records! (And don't be hurt if he or she shrugs and says no thanks.)

TERRIFIC PHRASES TO USE WHEN YOU'RE NO LONGER IN THE KNOW

I have no opinion about that. What do you think?
Go see ——; he/she is the expert on that.

Gosh, I've moved on and no longer maintain that info.

Thanks for thinking of me, but I'm not current on that anymore.

Sorry, I'm concentrating on finishing [my job task 1, 2, or 3] and just don't have time to find that stuff for you.

Wow, I didn't know that! Fill me in! (*Note:* This is to be used during coffee breaks, or when you have nothing better to do.)

"I Won't Look Productive If My Workspace Isn't Piled Up."

Stop! Piles don't equal productive. Seek a successful role model right now. It might be a coworker, the head of the company, other successful business owners and managers, or a friend in your association. Notice how their workspace is arranged. There are plenty of exceptions, but generally successful people have a method for handling lots of information. They have a system for knowing what's important, and they use it. Their office may not be perfectly tidy. But it's organized. Use them to inspire you.

Exception: The Big Push.

Sometimes you have to let your office get messy for a few weeks while you finish a big project with a tight deadline. Don't beat yourself up. Just concentrate on what you have to do.

"I'll Spend More Time Looking for Information in the Future."

Groundless. You'll spend less time looking for what's important to you because it will be concentrated. You'll spend less time looking for information that's not so important because a new word has been added to your self-talk vocabulary: *No.* As in "No, [your name here], stop letting yourself be distracted. Get back to [job task 1, 2, or 3]."

"I'll Lose My Creativity and Become Some Kind of Neatness Freak."

Two different issues. Being creative is not the same as being overwhelmed by mess. You'll probably become more creative once the underlying frustration of looking for things is removed. And who says anything about becoming a neatness freak? It's perfectly OK to have piles. They are now piles of related information.

"My Office Mate Will Encroach on My Space."

Another real issue, but one that can be dealt with far more effectively by a heart-to-heart talk. Try this: "Office Mate, let's divide up the shelves, tables, drawers, etc. I'm on a cleanup campaign and want to be clear on what I can change without fouling you up. Also, would you please identify a shelf where I can put any of your stuff that I happen to find in my area? I'm really committed to having a workspace that is cleared off and doesn't distract me."

"I Won't Be Able to Look Busy."

The days of looking busy while fondly pawing through all your prior accomplishments are history. Today, successful people *are* busy. Times change, and you'd better change with them. The reason you're reading this book is to reinvent yourself. From here on, you pass your days doing work that makes you valuable to your organization.

"That Project Represents Years of Work, and I Like Having Those Boxes Around Me."

What you need to ask yourself is how much time has passed since the project started and/or was finished. If the project was never finished and the information is several years old, write your boss a memo asking what to do. Get a written response back that is authorization to either dump the stuff or send it to an archival area for storage. If the project is done, it probably makes sense to keep the information handy for a year or two. Get some boxes and store the material. Take a felt pen and mark clearly what's in the box, and the time frames. Check with your attorney, accountant, legal department, client, etc., if you're not sure what your storage requirement is.

LABELING BOXES

A box label might read:

Original Surveys Conducted _____ for XYZ Report Published _____. Name, Department, Company, etc. To be discarded on _____.

Idea: If the real reason you are keeping those piles is sentimental attachment (a perfectly valid reason), see if you can't get creative about ways to keep the memory while reducing the bulk. Can you frame the cover sheet of the report? Pin up a photo of the team? Bind the executive summary?

What fears can you add to this long list of imaginary woes? Everyone has concerns; good information managers work through them. Sit down right now and examine your list. See how real your fears are. Talk things over with your boss or wise coworkers. Look at the benefits of working through those fears once and for all. They are stopping you from becoming the terrific info master you could be.

RETENTION SCHEDULES

Do you know that lots of people have wrestled with what to do with old information? In fact, there is a tool available to help you make the decision. It's called a *retention schedule*. Following such a schedule will keep you in conformance with legal requirements for many of the documents you have lying around. Figure 4-1 is representative of a typical schedule.

Check with your accounting, tax, or legal professionals; company archivist; or records manager for a retention schedule that might be customized for your type of organization.

THE SECRET IS BALANCE

The secret to overcoming information overload is to seek balance. You need to balance too much and too little. Too old and too preliminary. Too expensive to maintain and too expensive to re-create.

There is no perfect way. There are no guarantees. If you have a plan and have thought things through, your decisions will be prudent, justifiable, and as good as any other human being's. That's all you can do.

THE DISCIPLINE OF THE THREE DS

You've worked through your fears. Your shoulders are back. Your wastebasket and recycle bin are ready. It's time to attack the leftovers. You have three choices:

(text continues on p. 37)

Figure 4–1. Page from a typical retention schedule. *Source:* American Pioneer, Inc.

Accounts payable ledgers and schedules............... 7 years

Accounts receivable ledgers and schedules............ 7 years

Bank reconciliations.. 1 year

Capital stock and bond records; ledgers,
    transfer registers, stubs showing issues
    record of interest coupons, options, etc............. Permanently

Cash books.. Permanently

Charts of accounts... Permanently

Checks (cancelled but see exception below)............ 7 years

Checks (cancelled for important payments,
    i.e., taxes, purchases of property, special
    contracts, etc. (checks should be filed with
    the papers pertaining to the underlying
    transaction)... Permanently

Correspondence (routine) with customers
    or vendors.. 1 year

Correspondence (general)................................... 3 years

Correspondence (legal and important
    matters only)... Permanently

Deeds, mortgages, and bills of sale...................... Permanently

Depreciation schedules...................................... Permanently

Duplicate deposit slips...................................... 1 year

Employee personnel records (after termination)...... 3 years

Employment applications.................................... 3 years

Expense analyses and expense distribution
    schedules.. 7 years

General and private ledgers (and end-of-year
    trial balances).. Permanently

Insurance policies (expired)................................ 3 years

1. Dump
2. Delay discarding
3. Defer, to read later

Let's explore these options.

Dumping

Sometimes it just plain makes sense to dump and/or recycle those piles in your office. Consider dumping information when:

- It is out of date, for example, over three years old. The way technology is changing, one year is probably even better. Such information is no longer current or reliable.
- The project has been abandoned or finished.
- The information is no longer one of your interest areas.
- The sources aren't exceptional. Magazine articles, newsletters, etc., date quickly and usually aren't valuable over the long term.
- Trends have changed. Dump last year's fad and buzzwords. And yes, your college textbooks might as well go. Sorry to tell you, but even libraries don't want old texts.
- Issues that change frequently. Environmental issues, safety requirements, and accounting standards all change. Relying on old sources will get you in trouble.
- Material is updated regularly. Old catalogs are dangerous. The parts are no longer stocked, the prices no longer valid, and the specs no longer current. Dump them.
- The material is old revisions. Any well-managed organization adds a date-and-revision level to important work, drawings, work plans, etc. If you are not doing this, start now. Then it's easy to check and make sure you are using the most current informa-

Idea: **Who can give you a ruling on what to do with this stuff? Do you need it in writing?**

tion. Unless you are the designated historian for this material, work only with the current version.

Delaying

Balance is the key. If you've thought about this item carefully and still aren't sure, it's OK to wait a bit. At a minimum, try grouping like information, label it as above, and box it. Shove the box into a corner where it can sit a year or two while you see if it is ever needed. Does it need permanent storage? Refer to your retention schedule.

Deferring

If much material in your workspace is unread, make a quick pass. If it relates to your five areas, keep it in the catch area. These are your priority reading areas. If the material is not current, dump it now. You have more important things to work with.

INTERESTING BUT UNRELATED INFORMATION: BROWSING

Once you are current on your five information priority areas, you want to expose yourself to new ideas. The better info master you become, the more time for this you will have!

Idea: **Review the Top Twelve Excuses again. Then look at this pile. Are you sure you can't do something with it?**

You certainly don't want to become narrow-minded and dull; some stuff you'll want to read just because it is interesting, inspiring, or of future interest. Set aside one bottom file drawer or top shelf for this material. You can even set up subject file folders if you wish.

After you are finished reading the material, either file it or just keep it in this area. As a practical matter, you will probably never refer to it again. But if it comforts you to have it handy just in case, that's perfectly OK. Create a space for it and get it out of your five concentration areas.

Tip: Limit the amount of area allotted for nice-to-have information.

When the nice-to-have information starts to overflow its space, it's time to either dump or tighten up your criteria.

HOW CAN YOU FIT IN YOUR BROWSING?

If you store such material next to your briefcase, it's easy to grab an inch of material off the top of the stack as you leave your office for an appointment. Then you can do your browsing:

- In your boss's office while waiting for him or her to get off the phone, return from an appointment, etc.
- One day a week on your lunch hour
- One day a week on the bus, train, or ferry commuting to work
- While waiting for dentist, doctor, and other appointments
- On airplanes and in airports
- In bed at night
- During boring television shows
- During boring meetings? Wrong! Why are you in a boring meeting? If it's one of your priority areas, it's not boring. If it's not in a priority area, you need to talk to the committee chair and rethink your involvement.

One thing you need to know is that successful information masters read every day. But if you can read one day a week for an hour or so, you're making progress and will make a steady dent in those piles.

Remember: Unread information is the same as no information. Just having it piled up isn't doing you any good!

AFTER-HOURS READING: AN ATTITUDE EXAM

Do you still equate reading with school, tests, and punishment? Do you dread studying that thick report? Everyone starts out with these tapes left over from student days. It's the same reason Friday night is such fun. But you're out of school now; reading is the way your competitors are staying current. Reading is a very good investment in your success. An hour a week would be a good start. Which TV rerun can you give up?

Is reading hard for you? Perhaps that's your next personal improvement area. Help exists. Puzzle over how you can get it.

Well, there you have it: principles for how you can manage yourself and the information that surrounds you. You have a plan, a vision, and an office that works.

But information is dynamic. It is always coming into and going out of your workspace. You're ready for specific tips on how you can tame the information flow. Time to turn the page and move on to Part II. But it's perfectly OK to take a break . . . from this book. So go on. Why don't you take your break by sorting through just one more stack? You'll feel so good, and it really won't take very long.

PART

MANAGING INFORMATION

Now that you've completed Part I (Managing Yourself) you're ready for Part II, on managing information.

I divide information into two parts:

Incoming
Outgoing

To overcome information overload, you need to master both.

Incoming information is just what it says: information that arrives, from many sources, including mail, phone, and computer.

Chapter 5 helps you manage ''hard copy'': physical information you can hold and touch, such as all those reports piled up on your desk.

Chapter 6 focuses on verbal, nonwritten information such as phone calls and conversations. And where would you be without computers and electronic information, the subject of Chapter 7?

Outgoing information is that which you create and share with others. True information masters don't add to the glut of unneeded, unwanted, or poor quality information. Chapters 8, 9, and 10 present tips on managing outgoing hard copy, verbal, and electronic info.

Part II helps you identify which sources of information are essential to your professional success and gives you suggestions for bringing them under control. Don't let yourself be overwhelmed; the secret is to concentrate on improving these areas one step at a time. Becoming an information master is a process, not an event!

Incoming Information Flows

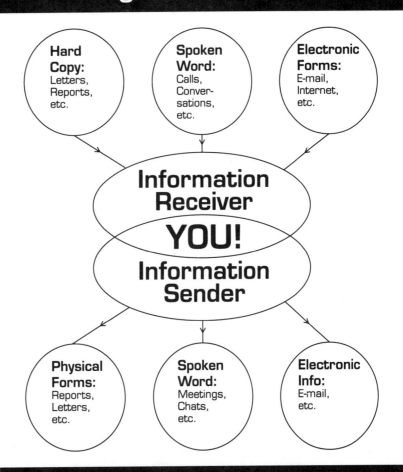

Hard Copy: Letters, Reports, etc.

Spoken Word: Calls, Conversations, etc.

Electronic Forms: E-mail, Internet, etc.

Information Receiver
YOU!
Information Sender

Physical Forms: Reports, Letters, etc.

Spoken Word: Meetings, Chats, etc.

Electronic Info: E-mail, etc.

Outgoing Information Flows

CHAPTER 5

CHANNELING THE DELUGE OF HARD COPY

Congratulations. Through concentrated effort, you have sorted and organized those piles that were once clogging your office. Like is grouped with like. You know what is important to you. You have dumped a lot of "stuff."

But you're nervous. You know your challenge is to maintain your system, processing new information as it comes in so you will never get behind again. The piles, stacks, and copies of information just never stop coming. As long as you can follow your daily routine, you're OK. But perhaps a big project is coming up that will take all your effort for a while. Or your really busy season is beginning, or you're doing a lot of travel. How can you stay on top of this never-ceasing flow?

If you are asking those questions, you have moved into advanced information management. The mere awareness of what will trip you up and cause you to slide backwards means you are well on your way to becoming an information master. This chapter offers assorted tips and suggestions for maintaining control.

HARD COPY

In this chapter we concentrate on the information that comes to you in hard form that you can hold in your hand. This category is huge. As you are well aware, you want to place your efforts on the information that is important to you: your five info priorities, including three job parts, plus self-improvement and future development areas. The question is: Is that the information you have in your office and receive on a regular basis?

Take an Incoming Info Inventory

One way to identify hard copy that is important to you is to first identify what your hard copy information is, by using the incoming info inventory (see Figure 5-1).

The simplest way is to get a new steno pad and plan on using one page per day. Date the page at the top. Figure you will track your info for a week or as long as needed to get a good feel for what hard copy is coming in with the mail, given out in staff meetings, and being hand-delivered.

List each piece of material on one line. Things you might want to note include:

> The type of item
> The sender
> Where you use (or don't use) the item
> Its scale of importance from A to D (D being unwanted
>   junk mail)

Don't worry about being perfect. All you want to do is get a good sense of:

- What is coming into your office. Are you really deluged with new information, or are you just overwhelmed by those piles of old stuff that you've never gotten around to processing?
- What material you get that you don't need. Duplicates? Courtesy copies?
- What information could go directly to someone else and bypass you in the future. An empowerment opportunity!
- What could come to you differently. Could you get by with the quarterly summary instead of weekly complication?

Figure 5-1. Incoming info inventory.

Date:	Type:	Sender:	Use:	Importance:
1/25:	Weekly Sales Projection	Jacob	Daily monitoring	A⁺
	Training Announcements (6 total) (Idea: Can HR post these instead of sending each person a copy??)	HR	Junk to me	C
	Company newsletter	PR Dep't.	Weekly update	B
	Customer service complaint reports (Note: This is 2 weeks late. Need to get my name on their "hot" distribution list.)	CS Dep't.	Monthly Summary Report	A
	Paycheck. Yeah!!	HR	Wish were daily!	A⁺
1/26:				

General categories you can use to start classifying include:

Reports: draft, final, summary, other
Correspondence: first-class letters, courier or priority, internal memos, incoming faxes, junk mail, other
Publications: professional journals, catalogs, general magazines, newspapers, books, other
Other information received: (add your own categories here) _____

_____

_____

YOUR GOAL: INCREASE WANTED INFORMATION

Late one Friday afternoon when you're too tired to start anything major, pull out these filled-out inventories and scan them. What sort of patterns do you see? Remember, if you aren't reading and using incoming information, it's doing you no good. Questions to ask yourself include:

1. Is what I absolutely must have coming to me routinely, or must I chase it down?
2. What steps can I take to make sure I get info in a timely fashion so I can do my work effectively?

YOUR GOAL: DECREASE UNWANTED INFORMATION

Yes, it's easy to mumble about junk mail and toss it quickly in the recycle bin. And maybe all those stacks on your desk even make you feel important. But you and your company are paying a price for handling all that info. The cost includes:

- Your time to make a decision about the worth of the material
- The cost to the administrative staff to get the mail to your desk (*Note:* If you're self-employed and have your own administrative staff, think what the real cost of handling that info is!)
- The cost to dispose of and/or recycle the info
- The higher product costs that are passed on to everyone

So why not bite the bullet and put a stop to what you don't want once and for all? Ask yourself: "What steps can I take on a one-time basis to reduce the flow of unneeded or wanted info permanently?" The following sections give two suggestions.

Internal Information

Return the unneeded courtesy copy, duplicate report, etc., with the following preprinted "delete note" stapled to it. Edit the note to make it sound like you. Type several copies onto one page. Run on bright paper. Cut into strips and have them ready beside your in basket.

> Dear Associate: I am committed to becoming an Information Master. To do that, I am concentrating on working with only that info which I absolutely must have to excel at my job. That means your valuable info isn't being used as it should be. Please delete my name from all distribution [or all but _____ (annual report, cover sheet, etc.)]. Thanks, [your name]
>
> P.S. Here's to saving trees, your efforts, and my time.

External Information

Tip: Batch the freebies you want to reject.

It's surprising how many different sources of external information you can think of in just a moment's reflection.

1. Freebies: Spend the postage to return your address label with a slash through it and the words *Please delete; no interest* scrawled across. Where to mail it? Look inside the publication on the first few pages for the small-print listing of where to send circulation requests.

Let the requests pile up for a month or so, and then take cheap envelopes and a stack of labels with you on an airplane. Doing a batch makes you feel so virtuous.

Be sure to complete and return "no interest" or "please delete my name" postcards whenever they are provided by the sender to gain time in the future.

Idea: Can you pay a teenager 25 cents per envelope to address them?

2. Paid subscriptions to magazines, professional journals, etc. Take a hard look every time they come up for renewal. Only subscribe to those that meet your goals, which means you read them and they cover your priority areas.

3. Daily newspapers. Ask yourself:

- Do you really read the newspaper every day, or does it just pile up? If you are recycling unread piles every week, perhaps it's time to stop your subscription and purchase a copy as your time permits.

- Can you share subscriptions?
- Can you make this on-the-bus reading?

Be aware that of all information producers, newspaper publishers have the least time to process and analyze information that will be useful for you. Fun reading, yes. But very few professions depend on daily newspapers for reliable info.

DON'T GET BEHIND! SORT DAILY

Process information every day. Small steps are the key to staying on top of the information avalanche. You've worked so hard to identify what is important to you. Now get creative about how you can carve out just a few minutes a day to do that initial sorting so you never get so far behind again. Your goal is to make sorting a habit, like locking up confidential papers at night. What small thing can you give up—such as chatting with someone who doesn't fascinate you—to pick up that few minutes needed to stay on top of today's incoming information?

FORM IS NOT IMPORTANT; CONTENT IS

Just because a fax is plopped on your desk by an out-of-breath administrative assistant who ran it down to you because it was marked "urgent," or just because something arrived express mail, doesn't mean you have to drop everything to respond.

Discipline yourself to finish your present task and then concentrate on the interruption.

Tip: Give your senders feedback.

If the senders routinely mark everything urgent, then nothing is urgent. Tell them you find their markings confusing and find yourself not looking at any of their stuff until you get around to it. Can you two agree on what *urgent* means? If the information or the request is coming from your boss,

Tip: Don't be overly influenced by how something looks.

can you negotiate priority flagging on time-sensitive items from him or her, so you don't have to drop everything unless it is really important?

Take a look at all the information on your list. Are you using the highest quality information possible? Can you stop using highly filtered information and instead use something closer to the original source? For example, read the book written by the author instead of assuming that a review is accurate.

Notice the appearance, but then take a hard look at the information itself. What is the level of detail? The qualifications of the author? The logic behind the opening sentences? Someone may be better at desktop publishing than at creating solid material!

THE ONE-FOR-ONE REALITY

If you have a job where you travel, accept the fact that it takes time to get organized once you return. You can do a preliminary sort very quickly. But if you have been gone a week, figure it will take you another week in the office to thoroughly review and process your important info. Do your thinking work while traveling and away from daily distractions. Savor your quiet time in hotel rooms.

Tip: Bring old envelopes on trips.

Bring lots of large recycled envelopes with you so you can sort the information you acquire during your trip into your five priority areas. Then you can do first passes quickly when you return.

LEARN FROM THE EXPERTS

If in spite of your best efforts you are stuck or keep falling behind, be aware that every type of problem you are struggling with has already been faced by many other people. And not only that, someone somewhere has written a book or developed a class expressly to help you figure out what to do.

Do not reinvent the wheel. Save your time for your priority areas. Once you are able to pin down the nature of your problem, such as lack of a filing system or poor time management, make it a self-improvement project to seek out a resource that should work for you. Your goal is not to become an efficiency expert. Your goal is to master five information areas.

KEEP REMINDING YOURSELF TO THROW THINGS AWAY

Just remind yourself that you need to keep very little. Make sure you don't drift. Keep only what you need to work with.

So far you've concentrated on controlling the physical information you can see and touch. Chapter 6 takes you to the more subtle information you hear but can't see or touch. What on earth do you do with that? Turn the page and find out.

CHAPTER 6

THE SPOKEN WORD: ORGANIZING INVISIBLE INFORMATION

You're doing great. Your old piles, stacks, and files are divided among your five priority areas, boxed for possible disposal, or in low-priority reading or storage shelves. Take a deep breath, a sigh of satisfaction. One big job is done.

Now sit down in your office chair and get ready to manage the next information source, one that is more subtle, not so easy to touch, move around, or throw away. But it is just as rich a source of valuable knowledge and just as time consuming as reports and printouts.

Invisible information is that which comes to you through your ears. It's all the things you hear. Invisible verbal information is powerful because in addition to content, you can often determine the emotional state of the talker. You can hear frustration, anger, enthusiasm, or certainty.

Even though you don't have hard copy to work with, verbal information needs to be managed just as much as those stacks you just finished sorting.

TAKE AN INVISIBLE INFO INVENTORY

Before you can organize and make maximum use of your invisible information, you have to know what it is. If this is a new concept to you, completing the inventory in Figure 6-1 over the next week or so is a good first step. Then you will *know* what information you work with, rather than

53

guessing. In many jobs such as sales and customer service, processing verbal information can involve enormous amounts of time.

To take your inventory, you have a choice. You can either start one steno pad and carry it with you for a week or so and note all conversations. Or you can use several, placing them beside various telephones, in your briefcase, and at your priority areas. In either case, fill out the pads as accurately as you can, but don't beat yourself up if you miss some days or conversations. Trends will become obvious even if your collection isn't perfect.

Time to put away this book for a week. Concentrate on your work and on being an independent observer. Just where is your time going? Where is your information coming from? Hmmm—should be fun to find out. Bet you uncover some surprises!

Remember that you are concentrating on information that is coming to you. Later in this book you learn how to manage all the verbal information you create and share with others.

Question: Can't decide whether you or your associate is the creator? Something appears mutually created? *Answer:* That's easy. One time add it to this form, and the next time leave it off. That way things should average out. There's no need to spend a lot of time sweating any one entry. You're a smart person and your "guesstimate" will be just fine.

Categories to get you started classifying include:

- One-on-one conversations: meetings, interviews, professional gossip shared, social conversations, other
- Conversation with two or more people: meetings attended, meetings chaired, other
- Incoming telephone calls: calls received, recorded messages received, recorded messages received from others, e-mail messages received
- Other: audiotapes played, fire drills

Figure 6-1.   Invisible info inventory.

Date:	Type:	Sender:	Use:	Importance:
2/25	Phone Call	Cold call	None	D
	"	"	"	"
	"	"	"	"
	"	"	"	"
	"	"	"	"
	"	"	"	"
	"	"	"	"

Note: Appear to be on sort of "hot list" for investments. Need to tell each caller to take me off call list!

	Phone call	Cecil	Hot prospect	A
	"	Farig	Unhappy customer	A
	"	Karen	Close deal	A
	Daily Staff Meeting	All staff	Production planning	B

Note: Could I reduce frequency?

	Phone call	Nelson	New product launch	A
	"	Juan	"	B
	"	Barb	"	C
	"	Bob	"	A
	"	Raddo	"	B

Note: This phone tag is ridiculous. There's got to be a better way to arrange this new product kick-off!! What is it??

(*Note:* Since for many people e-mail supplements the telephone, you might as well treat it the same as an incoming phone call for now. We discuss e-mail further in Chapter 7.)

WHAT HAVE YOU LEARNED?

Is your week up? Gather all your inventory forms and carve out another quiet hour for yourself. Make some rough tallies and look for trends. There are several things you can learn from these forms. There is no right or wrong answer. The main thing is not to kid yourself. If you don't like some of the things you discover, you don't need to tell anyone. Just make some changes.

INVISIBLE INFORMATION TRENDS

Ask yourself the following:

1. *Is at least 80 percent of the invisible information coming into your workspace related to your five priority areas?* If yes, that's great! It means your priorities are clear and you are concentrating your efforts where it matters to you. Treat those calls seriously, and return them promptly. The exchange of information between you and the caller is important stuff.

If no, then take a hard look. Are you on a one-time project that will end soon so you can get back on track? Or are some other forces at play? For example, is the reason you are overloaded that you are the office social center? If so, perhaps it's time to say no or find ways to pull yourself out of the loop. It's nice to be liked and popular. But as resources tighten, downsizing is implemented, or promotions are reviewed, you will be less competitive than others who stay focused on what they are paid to do.

Question: What about your nonpriority message sheets, which are piling up? *Answer:* Chapter 9 will address the subject of outgoing information, including phone calls, in detail.

2. *Is more than 95 percent of your invisible information work-related?* Yes? Take a hard look at your social skills. You could be missing a real opportunity to gather social information that could help you do your job better. Maybe it's time for you to reach out to others so you can get on the inside track occasionally. Why not call someone for lunch or volunteer for a special holiday project? Go on, pick up the phone now.

No? If you're receiving 80–95 percent priority-related information, you're working hard but still in the know!

3. *Do you have a system for using your invisible information the same way you use your hard-copy reports, printouts, etc.?* There are two types of invisible information that affect your work: obvious and subtle. Let's look at each of them.

Obvious Information

Obvious information includes things like statistics, quotes, dates, and other missing pieces of information that you need to do your work. Ask yourself these questions before relying on verbal info:

- What are the chances you misunderstood the message?
- Is the risk major if you are wrong, or is this a detail?
- Do you need to request hard-copy backup?
- Is this info essential to your priority areas such that you need to arrange to receive hard copy on a regular basis?

Tip: Store your invisible information the same way you do the hard copy for your five priority areas.

You can store messages and notes in file folders, in labeled envelopes, or taped to relevant reports. Remember: Put them where you will see them when doing that particular task. A forgotten message is the same as no message at all.

Subtle Information

This includes all the nuances, emotional overtones, and social or off-the-record juicy stuff that is part of every workplace. Working with it is a balancing act because you don't want to participate in the spread of malicious or damaging information that doesn't make your workplace pleasant. On the other hand, subtle information can be very useful. For example, if you heard in the lunchroom that someone is requesting a transfer, then perhaps you won't invite them to be on your committee because all their valuable work will have to be redone. *Important:* You need to check out the information by talking to the person yourself.

PERSONAL CONVERSATIONS

Personal conversations are about family, hobbies, sports, and your great weekend. Remember that

every time you are involved in personal conversations—whether you are talking or listening to
someone else—one of your five priority areas is
being neglected. Unless you have one of those un-
usual jobs in which you are rewarded for receiving
and acting on personal information (for example, a
gossip columnist), discipline yourself to concentrate on what you have already decided matters.

Information masters know they cannot be all
things to all people. They are there for a select
group of close friends, or in an emergency. They
are not parents, coaches, or sounding boards to
everyone who wants to talk.

If you are a part of a conversation about why
somebody is soooo busy or why something cannot
be done, quietly slip away. Thirty minutes from now
those people and those conversations will have
gone nowhere. You'll be thirty minutes closer to
your goals.

FOUR WAYS TO STORE INVISIBLE INFORMATION

Your goal is to develop a system that works for you. Here
are a few thoughts to inspire you.

1. A steno pad with one sheet per day works great if
   you need a chronological sequence to your messages
   and conversations and mostly use one phone. But be
   sure to date each page. The downside is that you
   don't have a way to move the information to your
   priority areas.
2. Spiral-bound message pads with NCR (no carbon
   required) second pages are handy. Then you can tear
   off the top sheet and move it to your priority storage
   area. The downside is that the little boxes on the
   forms for information entry don't hold very much.

3. Recycled paper beside each phone works great if you don't receive a lot of critical information. The information is easy to move around. The downside is those sheets can get easily lost.
4. Good calender systems have forms designed for recording conversations in meetings and hallways. Treat them the same as phone message sheets.

Note: If you observe that the telephone is a real obstacle to your success, make it a self-improvement project. There are some terrific books on telephone skills in your local bookstore.

Caution: Anything you put in writing can have legal ramifications. If you are documenting some sort of problem, be sure to get good advice from an attorney, the human resources department, etc.

Idea: Have fun! Tape record your phone messages every time you get an order or message of congratulations. Play it back during the weeks your phone doesn't ring.

You're ready to move to Chapter 7 and managing electronic information. Congratulate yourself on your progress. You are clearer now about what invisible information is important to your job success; you are receiving what you need to know; and you no longer feel so overwhelmed. Turn the page!

CHAPTER 7

ELECTRONIC INFORMATION: INCOMING BEEPS, BITS, AND BYTES

You've mastered hard copy and the invisible information that you receive through your ears. Just one big category left, and that is electronic information: what is displayed via the flickering CRT, the computer monitor sitting on your desk. The electronic age is increasing the flow of information into your professional life. Talk about an area where you can never know it all! Electronic information needs to be managed the same as any other.

What, you've not yet joined the computer age? No problem. Just skim this chapter as part of your future development.

ELECTRONIC INFORMATION SOURCES

Electronic info comes to you from different sources. It's time for another survey so that you can identify which sources are important and where you need to place your effort. Feel free to adapt this form so that it works for you. Remember, you're not defending a Ph.D. dissertation; you're just getting perspective so you can reduce information overload and do good work.

The sources you will review in this chapter include:

- Application programs: those workhorses you use every day to write letters, create statistics, and design newsletters

- Information you insert: including CD-ROMs, floppy disks, tapes, etc.
- Linkages to other computers: e-mail, the Internet, the Web, groupware
- Television, videotapes, and other video

Please note: This is not a book about computers. If your system is powerful and well organized, just review this chapter and reward yourself for being an expert. If, however, after reading this chapter you realize computers are essential to your work and your system is outmoded, you may want to make it a personal-improvement project to upgrade your capability.

APPLICATION PROGRAMS

You know the routine: You need to collect some basic information before you can manage it. Pick a period of time such as a week, if that represents your typical job, or a month if you have an irregular schedule. Create a copy of the form in Figure 7-1 and put it beside your computer along with a clock so you can note elapsed time. Keep a log of how you actually use your computer.

When your data collection time period is up, sit down with your reports and do the following:

- Rank-order your most important application programs. Ask yourself: Are you proficient at operating these programs, or do you need to increase your efficiency through a personal-improvement project? Is your computer your most important information-processing tool? If so, get good at it! The investment in yourself will pay back for years to come.
- What other programs are installed on your hard drive? Have you used them in the last year? Do they slow up your running speed? Are they hogging memory? Are there any programs to delete?
- What else can you observe about the way your computer is configured? Is your physical arrangement

Figure 7–1. Computer applications inventory.

Application Programs on My Computer

Date:	Use:	Word Processing	Spreadsheet	Desktop Publishing	Database	Inventory Management	Production Planning
2/18:	New brochure draft			1 hr			
	Update address changes				1 hr		
	Letters & notes	2 hr					
2/19:	Computer dead!						
2/21:	More brochure drafts			3 hr			
	Newsletter						
2/23:	Purchasing updates					4 hr	4 hr

comfortable and convenient? Any chance of repetitive stress injuries? What is working well? Are your current manuals and "cheat sheets" easy to grab? What do you need to work on? What software bugs inconvenience you? Any hardware crashes?

SIDEBAR: TOUCH TYPING

If you never learned how to touch type (or "keyboard," if you went to a progressive school), *learn now.* There are several reasons why this will be one of the best investments in yourself you can make.

1. Touch typing is easy to learn. Within a few weeks you can have the basic skills. Then your

proficiency will build every time you do your work. Resources include software tutorial programs, community colleges, business schools, your company's training department, and bookstores.

2. "Hunt and peck" makes you appear to others as behind the times, slow to produce work, reluctant to learn, afraid of technology, and not prepared for the future. Even if you can type fast hunting and pecking, this is true. You want your fundamental computer skills to be adequate so that when future opportunities come up you aren't discounted as being behind the times.

3. Your productivity will increase once your brain can fully concentrate on entering and retrieving information instead of on watching the keyboard.

4. Proper techniques will lessen your risk of repetitive stress injuries. Unless you are retiring this year or have a job that will never require you to use a computer (belly dancer? limo driver?), learn to touch type. Becoming an information master requires this vital, easy-to-learn skill.

SOFTWARE UPGRADES

Software upgrades, like all information, are limitless. The cost isn't the few dollars to purchase the program. The cost is in your time to learn the new commands, convert your files, and reconfigure your computer.

Consider upgrades when:

- Your present program is an early version with bugs.
- You have mastered the present program and want to do more complex functions.

- You are acquiring a new, more powerful computer system.
- You have identified this program as a future improvement project, and mastering the latest version will increase your competitive edge.

Consider waiting to upgrade if:

- You have mastered your present program, it works fine, and it does 90 percent of what you need.
- Learning this new program does not relate to one of your priority areas.
- Your buddies are bragging about a hot new program they just installed and you feel left out. (*Note:* This is an ego thing, and it's tough not to be leading-edge. Just listen or ask questions, and remember your focus.)
- You have a better use for the money for the upgrade costs and/or the time.

ORGANIZING YOUR COMPUTER HARD DRIVE

If your computer hard drive, application programs, and data contained are not organized into subdirectories, trees, batch files, and paths, then hire, bribe, or trade with a techie to help you out. You don't necessarily have to learn how to do this yourself. But a one-time investment in the organization of your hard drive will definitely accelerate your path to info master.

This type of investment will also lend order to your floppies and backup system. Remember, losing valuable information is the greatest waste of your time because it is so unnecessary. Computers crash. Expect it. Prepare for it.

INFORMATION YOU INSERT

This is a catch-all category of information that you add to your computer. Not everybody does this; it depends on the nature of your work. The three basic types of inserted information are floppy disks, CD-ROMs, and backup tapes.

Floppy Disks

If you have the type of job in which you receive information from others via floppy disks, then you will want to incorporate the control of this information in your priority-management system.

Examples include floppies from:

- Consultants such as engineers or marketers who prepare work for others
- Commercial sources such as databases for mailings
- Text written by someone else for which you are in charge of formatting and printing

Even though these may not be original source documents, treat them with care and store them in your three job-part areas.

Caution: Every time you load a floppy disk that has been in somebody's else's computer, there is a risk of introducing a virus into your computer. Run your antivirus programs frequently.

CD-ROMs

CD-ROMs look like gold or silver records, and they contain an incredible amount of information. Think of them as books—make that encyclopedias!—on disk. Newer computers come with CD-ROM drives built in. Perhaps you can upgrade your system and add one if you wish. CD-ROM technology is expanding rapidly and is one that good information masters monitor.

The good news is most reference CD-ROMs can be searched by key words. The bad news is they get obsolete just as books do.

Question: What sort of a system do you have for upgrading your CD-ROMs?

Caution: No electronic medium, including CD-ROM, is as dense with information per screen as a book page. Notice how you can quickly skim a book page. Notice how much more information it contains than a computer screen. CD-ROMs are but one of many information sources. This statement is worth repeating. Ignore the form, and concentrate on content, even if it isn't the latest hot stuff.

Tapes

Tapes can be in the form of audiotapes you play in your car or while jogging. They are great for making the miles pass on long trips. You may also have a tape system built into your computer for backup. There's not much for me to add that you don't already know how to do.

LINKAGES TO OTHER COMPUTERS

If you are networked to other computers or use a modem to receive e-mail or cruise the Internet, then you are linked to and receiving info from other computers. Congratulations, you are at the forefront of the information age.

If you and your computer are self-contained and do not have any connection to other computers, then this section will not pertain to you—or not yet. Just read it to understand a few of the buzzwords.

E-mail: Having messages waiting for you in your computer in basket is as much fun as opening the mail. E-mail also contains about the same percentage of junk mail. Each on-line system is different, but here are a few general tips for managing e-mail.

INCOMING E-MAIL TIPS

1. Process your e-mail in batches. You don't open each letter as it comes in! You do them all at once and follow good techniques, just as with postal mail: making quick decisions and handling each piece as little as possible. Do the same with your e-mail. Accessing e-mail twice a day is reasonable.
2. Give your important contacts key words so you can sort by those key words and know at a very quick glance that their message is something important.
3. Clean out your mailbox every day. Step by step is the key. Otherwise the pile gets so depressing you keep procrastinating and never get really caught up. Trade with a colleague to do a rough sort and clean out while each of you is on vacation.
4. Take active steps to take yourself out of any loop of information that is not one of your priority areas. *Do it now.* The e-mail information explosion has just begun. Give up any fantasy of keeping "nice to know" info coming in.
5. Don't overreact to nuance in an e-mail. Many people are not very good writers and inadvertently use language that can be misconstrued. Get on the phone and ask for clarification rather than becoming paranoid or letting things escalate into a real misunderstanding.

CRUISING THE INTERNET AND THE WORLD WIDE WEB

The Internet is a worldwide hookup of computers via telephone lines. You can receive information from libraries, schools and universities, government agencies, and other businesses. The Web is a way of accessing graphics such as pictures and images in addition to plain text. The power of both systems is that they are interactive. You can communicate via your computer with people and organizations all over the world.

The question to ask yourself is, Do you need a worldwide hookup to other people, businesses, and computers? The Internet is well worth your time if:

- You are research based, such as a scholar or market researcher.
- Your competitive edge requires you to measure and respond in minutes or days to what your competition is doing. People who work in certain international financial markets fit here.
- Your business is computer linkages and related spinoffs.

If you don't fit those categories, ask yourself whether you really have to be on the "bleeding edge" of new technology.

Note that standards for the Internet are not yet established. That means both the hardware and software will be changing rapidly in a very short period of time. If you want to be on the front of the wave, fine. But do it consciously and with an established goal of future benefit to you.

Caution: The linkage of computers is causing an information explosion. If you are not disciplined, you can spend hours and hours of your valuable time on information that is nice to know or fun, and fail to complete your priority areas. Remember, you must make information work for you because you will never know it all.

Possibilities:

- Can you make computer linkages a future development area and schedule a time to master it?
- Can you explore it at night instead of watching TV?
- Can you hire an expert to cruise for you? To teach you?

Here's an important concept to grasp: Cruising the Internet is "on-demand." That means you go to it; it doesn't come to you unless you make it. You are in control. If you don't log on, you aren't overloaded!

Groupware is the term used for a special set of network linkages usually found in big organizations in which a number of people are electronically queried or surveyed at once. Everyone involved is asked the same questions and has an opportunity to send messages of response to a central collection and analysis point. It greatly speeds up communication and increases individual involvement without the time many meetings would take.

Groupware is powerful because everyone gets to respond, not only the most verbally skilled. If your company has groupware, make it work for you. This is your chance to provide input to those key questions and concerns being surveyed.

TV, VIDEOTAPES, AND MISCELLANEOUS SOURCES

One last source of incoming information is that which you receive from television shows, instructional videotapes, infomercials, and any other shows you may have occasion to watch, such as satellite hookups.

Although the information has a visual component that makes it compelling and entertaining, it still has to be interpreted and processed in your mind. How can you use or pass on the information in your work?

If you have a copy of the video, the best way is to treat it the same way you do information from conversations. Get out those specially designed forms of yours for recording conversations, and make notes as you watch. The good news is you have a backup copy available for replay or reference. Watching a video can be slow going, however, if the information is reasonably familiar to you.

What if you are watching a television show and want to use the information? Quick! Grab a piece of paper and note the time, channel, speaker, program name, and anything else you can get down. Then call the station and try to purchase the video, a transcript of the conversation, or at least confirm the details of the program. Although snobs may sniff, much current information is available on television through interviews with authors and special programming.

Store all videotapes according to their priority area. Label and date them. Discard per your retention schedule the same way you do other out-of-date publications.

Whew! No wonder you've been overloaded. Information has been coming at you from many sources. You have to remember, sort out, and use not only reports and printouts but all those conversations and electronic transmissions. Aren't you smart to get control of your information now? As more information is created, you will stay in control. The secret of the information master is to keep nibbling away one step, one piece, one conversation at a time.

Time to turn the page: You're ready to stop adding to the glut of information.

CHAPTER 8

REDUCING THE GLUT:
HARD COPY

Now you're going to shift your attention from managing information that comes in to managing information that goes out. But first it's time to celebrate. Slowly rotate your chair and admire your workspace. Not only does it look organized (not perfect mind you, just organized), but it is truly an information center.

You have:

- Places for your three job priorities where all related information is concentrated, or at least cross-referenced
- Spots to collect information for your self-improvement and future-development projects
- Top shelves, bottom drawers, and corners where lesser information is stored
- A few labeled boxes hidden behind tables and in closets that you probably will dump in a year or so, once you reassure yourself that you never did need that material after all

JUST FOR FUN: LOOKING GOOD!

So far we've ignored cosmetics and appearances. But if your information is prioritized, now is the time to:

71

- Master that label printing program and make some nice-looking, descriptive labels for your hanging and manila files.
- Start a whole new series of different-colored file folders at the beginning of your next fiscal year or big project.
- Put description cards on the outside of your file drawers and bookcases so your coworkers can find things when you're off work.
- Get rid of supplies that either don't work anymore or depress you. It's OK to spend a little money now in your local office supply store because you know what will work for you and you know your information management system, one that you have carefully designed. From here on you'll only be fine-tuning.
- Hire a professional organizer to help you smooth out your work flow if you are stuck. If you now know your focus areas but find things are still messier than you would like, an expert can help.

But that's not all. Look how your work habits and productivity have improved. Now that you have your important information concentrated, you can:

- Finish a memo in one sitting because all the info you need is right at your fingertips. No excuses here. You do good work and you do it on time.
- Have fewer and shorter meetings, because more issues can be resolved the first time they come up. Key people eagerly attend your meetings because people know their time is well spent.
- Make solid recommendations that convince your boss and coworkers because your proposals are documented by clearly referenced materials.
- Sound more confident when speaking because the guesswork and uncertainty is gone.
- Warmly welcome visitors into your workspace,

knowing it looks professional. There's even an empty seat for them!

You can probably add other benefits to your particular list. Please do: Your efforts have given you a good return on your investment.

If you want to take a break for a bit and concentrate on a big project for one of your priority areas, feel free. You've earned a change of pace.

MANAGING THE NEXT PHASE: OUTGOING INFORMATION

But you're not an information master yet. No, your challenge now is to manage the information that leaves your workspace. This chapter concentrates on the physical stuff, the pages, reports, memos, and other hard copy you produce.

Remember the good old days, when you were feeling overwhelmed? One reason you felt so frazzled was because of all those well-meaning people who deluged you with information. But now the buck stops with you. Your goal is to be neither overwhelmed nor an "overwhelmer". You're right, that's not a word, but have fun with the concept!

The first question is, do you need to create this information at all?

GUIDELINES: PUT IT IN WRITING

As you take responsibility for the information you create, you ask yourself, Should this information be distributed in written form? A more fundamental question is, Should this information be generated at all?

Let's assume you're beyond busywork and the value is unquestioned. Here are some guidelines. Put it in writing when:

- Legal or other formal documentation is required. A written reprimand in a personnel file is an example.
- The subject is complicated and misunderstanding will be reduced by having things in writing. A safety procedure for operating complicated machinery is an example.
- Hard copy is going to be required sooner or later, either for storage or distribution. Examples include policies or guidelines. If that is the case, you might as well start preparing drafts for discussion.
- You want to control the nature of the information. There is power in the interpretation of your pen (or laptop computer). Offer to draft an agreement or contract. Then you'll know what's in it.
- Multiple copies will need to go to people. Broadcast fax, for example, can be an efficient way to inform all committee members.
- Details could be misunderstood. Date, time, place, directions, maps, and agenda items are good stuff to put in writing.
- You are creating a history or reminder for infrequent events that you or others will refer to in the future. This can be in the form of Notes to the File. Doing a brain dump can reduce much wasted effort the next time your successor struggles with their first international shipment, for example.
- You want to CYA. That is an old army term that means—well, let's just say you want to cover your posterior in case a situation goes bad. You certainly don't want to be a whiner or holier-than-thou. But there are times when it is prudent to note your position.

Feel free to add to this list. But before you do, take a look at suggestions for when *not* to put things in writing:

- When you are angry and the finger-pointing and accusations could come back to haunt you later.
- When the information isn't worth the effort it takes to write it. Writing takes time. Would a phone call do?

- When your spelling or grammar skills are poor. What if your reader is a crossword puzzle addict or an English literature freak? Or someone who cares about appearances? Regardless, your message will be discounted. Don't set yourself up.

DON'T BE BITTEN BY THE POORLY WRITTEN REPORT

Simple test: If you don't know when to use *it's* versus *its*, if you're talking about a *principle* or a *principal*, or the difference between *lay* and *lie*, your written materials could hurt you. Whether you hated English in high school or English is a second language for you, in some professions poor writing skills will limit career opportunities. Generally speaking, jobs with greater responsibilities—and greater money—require you to communicate in writing.

What to do?

- Make improving your English skills one of your self-improvement projects. Take classes or buy books. You can learn this. Nobody was born fluent in English!
- Ask a professional secretary to review your written materials before you print final copies. *Question:* How can you help him or her out, too?
- Trade reviews with a coworker, and then do something for him or her. (Bosses can really help, if you don't have one who will penalize you for your lack of skills at review time.)
- Collect samples of work in your company that seem to be widely regarded as excellent or acceptable. Use them as standards and guidelines.
- Use handwriting. This is thin, but your reader

> might assume you were in a hurry instead of un-
> able to write!
> - Change careers.
> - Increase another skill to such a level that your
>   poor grammar is tolerated. For example, if you
>   can get the computer network to switch print-
>   ers or find files after a hard-drive crash, people
>   will happily edit your letters!

GUIDELINES FOR SHARING INFORMATION

Have you considered the possibility that your carefully crafted report is junk mail? Well, it is. That is, it's junk if the receiver doesn't want or need the info.

Why do you care what impact information you send out has on others? Because you want you, your work, and the information that is a reflection of you to be treated with the respect you have earned.

Here's a test of what ideally should happen to information as it leaves your office. How do you and your information measure up?

1. Hard copy goes *directly* to people for whom the subject is one of their job-priority areas. (How do you confirm this? Ask them!)
2. Hard copy goes *promptly* to those same people. (If you're finished writing but too busy to distribute copies, you're not finished.) *Note:* If you send copies to some people before others, you're playing politics. Be sure you know what you're doing.
3. Courtesy copies go only to those who have requested them or have a specific need to know. (Do you review this list quarterly? Use a positive-response postcard or other form of confirmation.)
4. You have one-page executive summaries available for those with general or marginal interest.

5. Everything that leaves has date of preparation, date of expiration, any company reference numbers that are needed, all signoffs and authorizations, and your name and title.
6. If something is either draft or confidential, that is clearly stamped on the cover and/or all pages if necessary.
7. If you use mailing lists, they are updated at least once a year.

EGO, NUMBERS, AND PRESS RELEASES

Info masters don't kid themselves that quantity equals quality. If you mail 1,000 copies of a complete report, of which 950 go immediately into the circular file, you've effectively mailed 50 copies. And how many of those get read in any detail? Yes, of course this is the greatest information ever produced—or so it seems to you. But set your ego aside and look at things from the receiving end: Remember what cascades into your office every day. You are one of many. Might as well accept it.

Here's another reality. Both paper and postage are too expensive to continue to mail to "the world." Those 950 copies represent money and effort that could be spent better somewhere else. And what about trees and landfills? Doesn't your conscience hurt?

Your goal as an info master is to make the job of your recipients easy. How? Filter the information for them. Remember how you sort your own information: A page or two has a chance of ending up in your browse pile, but at five or more pages you shrug and toss it as too heavy to lug around or too long to wade through. That's life in the day of cheap laser printers, folks.

Press releases—a form of the one-page executive summary with a contact person and phone number added—are the way to tell the world about your great work. Add a line about how to obtain complete copies. Send this instead of the entire report. Then those who really want the information will seek it out. And you might even get an article in a journal or newspaper. That's the way to get the great exposure you were really seeking!

Universities and governments have traditionally used wide distribution channels and measured success in numbers. If you work for one of them, be brave and speak up. Question whether it might be time to reinvent yourselves by taking a look at the distribution list—preferably before a committee of the legislature does it for you. Perhaps you could even volunteer to chair the project.

WRITING AS REFLECTION OF THOUGHT

This chapter has sought to show you how to reduce information overload. You've learned that a good information manager questions the use and contribution of what he or she sends out. You've acquired tips for what to put in writing and how to distribute your written materials.

But before you go on, play philosopher for just a minute. Think about how powerful the ability to write is.

Writing is the way you express your expertise to other people . . . using just twenty-six letters! What geniuses those alphabet inventors were. Few people can write well. The reason is that describing actual events using words is difficult for almost everybody. You're dealing with concepts and abstractions instead of things or actual experiences.

Perhaps increasing your ability to express yourself in writing doesn't need to be an immediate self-improvement project. Overcoming information overload is a tremendous accomplishment for you for this year. But file away in your subconscious the fact that whenever you are ready to advance into top management and big money, your writing skills will need to be, at a minimum, "acceptable." Once you need to present information to more than a few people at once on a face-to-face basis, it's time to improve your ability to use those twenty-six letters.

Enough heavy stuff. On to reducing verbal glut.

CHAPTER 9

LOWERING THE BABBLE: CALLS, CONVERSATIONS, AND MEETINGS

Of course you love to talk. And your conversations are brilliant. That's not in question. But every time you talk you are creating outgoing information that adds to a coworker's overload. Your challenge is to be sure you are managing this information the best way possible.

Here is what you master in this chapter:

- Pros and cons of talking
- Personal conversations: yes or no
- Optimizing use of phone calls
- Making optimal use of meetings

PROS AND CONS OF TALKING

Did you know it is far faster for most people to read words than to speak them? It is also faster to read words than to listen to them being spoken. Experiment. Read this paragraph out loud. Notice how your eyes can easily get ahead of your speech. There are exceptions, and if you have a reading disorder you certainly know that. But as a general rule, it is faster to read a page than to listen to the same information presented via a conversation.

Just for the heck of it, try this the next time you are in a hotel room or other public facility whose television sets have closed captions available for the hearing impaired. Use the remote control to turn the option on. Then watch a talk show. In addition to the regular conversations you continue to hear, you will have the words written across the bottom of the screen. Rather like a foreign film with subtitles. Notice whether or not you finish reading while the two people are still talking. Most people do.

What does this mean to you as an information manager? It means reading a report is faster than having someone present it to you in a meeting.

Of course there is a downside to the written word too. For one thing, it is more time-consuming to write than to talk. The emotional nuances are missing; the information exchange is one way. And it's a lot less fun. As with all information, balance is the key.

PERSONAL CONVERSATIONS: YES OR NO

When you have information to convey, here are some questions to help you decide whether to talk or write. Notice they are only guidelines; you will apply the final judgment. Remember the consciousness-raising sessions of the sixties? That's what you're doing here: raising your conscious awareness of your options.

Question number one: Does the information need to go to more than one person? If so, then writing probably makes more sense. Why make five phone calls to tell people about a meeting when writing down the details once and mailing them to each party will save time and reduce misunderstandings?

Question number two: Is the information of a sensitive nature? Here is where personal conversations shine.

First, a heart-to-heart talk is your chance to express your caring and concern. Your voice adds an entire dimension of emotion that written words cannot convey. Let's face it. At work you don't have the time to craft elegant prose, and it would be inappropriate even if you could. Picture it in a personnel file! No thanks.

Second, many misunderstandings can be eliminated before they escalate. Any errors or confusion are resolved immediately.

DISCUSSING SENSITIVE INFORMATION

Start by listing the many areas on which you and your listener both agree. You'll be amazed at how much common ground you do share.

Then raise the areas of disagreement point by point. You'll find they are more easily put into perspective and seen as a matter that you two smart people can creatively work out.

Remember your puzzle mentality from Chapter 1? Use it here. Your shared responsibility is to find a way to make things work.

Question number three: Is the information not worth the time it would take to write it? Remember, writing is slower than talking. You are the one doing the crafting. Is this issue worth the effort?

Question number four: Is the information of a time-sensitive or crisis nature? You don't write a memo about "Subject: fire burning in stockroom." You yell it out, and fast. Do the same thing for other crisis situations. For example, if you are in danger of losing a big order to a competitor, your boss probably wants to know *now*. That way you have more time to work together and save the order. A memo is too slow.

Question number five: Do you have a hidden agenda? Wanting to make a friend, looking for a chance to get acquainted with a new coworker, the possibility of getting advance information, an agreeable conversation with a peer with whom you often disagree . . . any of these subtle factors can be good reasons to stop that person for a brief chat.

Question number six: Does the information relate to a policy matter that will have to be put in writing sooner or later? Especially for complex issues, prepare a rough draft to focus your discussions.

Question number seven: Does your work involve a creative aspect in which two people could produce better information than one? In that case, bounce that idea off someone smart *before* spending a lot of time writing up a new product description.

CAUTION: TIME WASTERS

Now that you are an information master, you are careful not to get involved in conversations that are going nowhere. You just keep walking.

The other side of that is, don't start conversations that are going nowhere. For example, sharing early rumors about mergers or possible layoffs is rarely productive because you cannot take any action based on rumor. You might as well keep doing your job so you will be valuable no matter what happens. If a situation has to unfold over time before you can or will do anything about it, then stick to your focus areas.

Tip: Prepare a conversational agenda.

Do you prepare an agenda for conversations? Why not? It's a great way to make sure you get the information you need the first time, don't have to pester the person more than once, and look incredibly well prepared. It's really simple to do. Your agenda might look like this:

> See Judi today:
>
> Exact time of budget review
> Confirm Sang has seen proposed cuts

Get her opinion on chances for new computer system
Ask if daughter's chicken pox is gone!

Reminder: Do you need to document your conversation?

Chapter 8 had suggestions for putting things in writing as a form of closure. Conversations have to be finished, too. Part of that process is asking yourself, Do I need to document the record for future reference?

If so, do it. Title the paper Memo to File. Be sure to list the subject, add the date and time of the conversation, and who was involved, including yourself. Do *not* add personal comments, opinions, or observation that could be misconstrued or that you cannot prove. Documented conversations can be used in court. Make them professional.

OPTIMIZING OUTGOING PHONE CALLS

Telephone calls follow most of the same guidelines as personal conversations. They are one-on-one, they're quick to make, they don't involve writing, and they're cheap.

There is one *big* difference. Emotional aspects of a conversation can be misconstrued over the telephone. The phone call loses the supplemental information you gain from facial expressions and body language. For example, fatigue in a voice can easily be mistaken for lack of interest. A hesitation in the voice caused by swatting away a fly could be heard as reluctance to support a request.

If the subject is sensitive or confrontational, meet in person. If by some chance you know you are "off" that day, explain that. For example you might say, "Gosh, I've been working a lot of overtime. Forgive me if I sound low on energy."

Tip: Write while you talk on the phone.

If you make any sort of telephone calls that involve updating a database, taking sales orders, or a similar type of work, teach yourself to keyboard notes into the computer as you talk. Don't get in the habit of writing notes on a piece of paper that will have to entered later.

The trick is to have the computer up and the right program running before you make any calls. It also means you position your telephone and keyboard side by side, use a headset so your hands are free, and do whatever else it takes to make it easy to listen and type.

Fortunately, you've already become a crack typist so this is just a further upgrade of your future development skills. Hunt-and-peck is too slow for this type of update.

Question: Do you make voice mail work for you?

Voice mail and message machines are a way of life. Use them to strategically make your phone calls. You can schedule your calls when you have a good chance of finding someone *in*—or when you have a good chance of finding someone *out*. You'd like to find someone in when:

- You want to quickly resolve a matter.
- You have serious issues to discuss.
- You know the person will take your call.

You want to find someone out when:

- They would probably refuse to take your calls (a sad reality for many salespeople).
- You want to leave a message without interruption. That's the power to the caller of most voice mail: People have to listen to your entire message once.
- You're passing on details that don't justify interrupting your associate's train of thought.
- It's after hours, the rates are cheaper, and a message will do.

Caution: With so many people working at home, all you East Coast folks should be certain you are not interrupting the sleep of your West Coast customers. A cheery phone message placed at 8:00 A.M. in New York is received at 5:00 A.M. in California. If the business line is on a desk in the bedroom . . . well, you get the idea.

OPTIMIZING USE OF MEETINGS

If a conversation is the verbal sharing of information between two people, a meeting is the verbal sharing of information with three or more people.

Tap the Power of Meetings

Meetings can be a great way to pass on knowledge, give direction, build camaraderie, and encourage teamwork. If the right people attend and you as chair are a pro at running the meeting, you and all attendees leave energized and focused. Staff meetings, sales presentations, and budget reviews are institutions of American business. When well run, they can be a great use of everybody's time.

But knowledge, teamwork, direction, and camaraderie are not where the power of meetings lies. The real justification for a meeting is when the subject is complex and the collective mental power of the group can be tapped to come up with proposals and solutions that one or two people alone couldn't generate. The synergy of having everyone concentrate on resolving a situation can be incredibly productive. Examining all the different perspectives at one time can also shortcut future concerns long before they ever cause serious problems.

Tip: Don't let the verbally skilled (i.e., big talkers) dominate.

You want information from those who don't talk as much but have valuable experience. Make a point to go around the room, giving everyone a chance to comment on important points.

A Note on Brainstorming

Brainstorming is a formal technique for removing boundaries and thinking very creatively. Presented with a situation, people throw out the most creative solutions they can think of. Objections are not allowed. By definition, brainstorming is not limited by available information and takes outcomes beyond the realm of the practical.

You may or may not want a brainstorming aspect to your meeting. It is a powerful way to reinvent your assumptions. Consider trying it out when no options are appealing.

Tip: If you are going to brain-storm, make it a scheduled event.

Research how to do brainstorming right. A conversation full of aimless possibilities is not brainstorming. It's a waste of time.

Some tips on the information in meetings:

1. *Note taking.* For every meeting, designate a recorder to write down the information generated. If the group is small, your notes on a steno pad or your laptop computer may be enough.

Definitely use a designated note taker or professional secretary if:

The group is large

The discussion is complex

The procedures and record must be formally documented

Good ideas will be lost

2. *Audiotaping.* Tape recording a meeting rarely works. Remember how slow the spoken word is? You'll have a hard time finding volunteers to sit through that tape and take notes. Also, taking notes from listening to a tape creates confusion over who is speaking. Sooner or later that information is going to have to be condensed and filtered. You might as well do it in the note-taking process.

3. *Know what to omit.* Advise your note taker what *not* to write down. Personal asides, witty but nasty cracks, and personal comments are best never put in the record.

4. *Avoid fragmented information.* Prepare a good agenda and stick to it. That is the key to running a good meeting, because then little irrelevant information is discussed. But do have a way to write down possibilities, concerns, and good ideas that occur to participants during the meeting.

Suggestion: Give each person a small note pad to write down nonagenda ideas or thoughts that occur to them. How about something fun, perhaps in the shape of a light bulb?

Time is your most valuable, nonrenewable resource. Actively controlling the information from conversations, meetings, and the phone calls you make is one of the most powerful contributions you can make to optimizing use of your time and that of your coworkers.

A final thought: You can almost always find a second chance to have a conversation. But you can never take words back. Make sure your words are spoken thoughtfully and caringly.

And now, on to bits, bytes, and glittering screens. How can you manage your outgoing electronic info?

CHAPTER 10

SLOWING ELECTRONIC GLUT

This is it! Just one last push and you will be an information master graduate.

Just look at how you have changed your life since you first picked up this book. Remember how overwhelmed you felt? How you used to beat yourself up over the mess? The missing documents? The hopeless nature of your office?

Look what you've done:

- You now have realistic expectations about what you can and can't do. You focus your energy on what matters, rather than letting it dissipate into . . . well, what did it go into? Time just passed.
- You're ready to take on a new self-improvement area, one that really matters to you, because now you can cross off your list overcoming information overload. If you've been diligent, these habits and this way of thinking are part of you. You're into maintenance of a system now—and that's far less demanding than construction.
- You have more time to do what's important to you. And you know what that is.
- The final exciting point is that you are free to grow and enjoy the future. You're continually exploring where your energy will go, and you're open to how to get there.

Enough reflection. Let's get back to work. Applying the ideas in this chapter shows you how to master the info you generate and send out electronically.

Although you receive all sorts of sophisticated electronic information, you probably don't create much. For most people, outgoing electronic information means the transmission of e-mail. Let's examine that.

THE ERRONEOUS ASSUMPTION: THE ELECTRONIC WAY IS ALWAYS BETTER

You're not a professional techie, so you have worked hard to master new technology. (Oops—you are a professional techie? Well, please be patient with the rest of us then!) You like being one of the "big kids" who isn't afraid of this new-fangled stuff. You look with pity at the old-timers who refuse to learn. By now you know how to send e-mail, hook up fax modems, visit a chat room, download files, and broadcast faxes. You feel like hot stuff. And you are!

But to keep the status of information master, you must continually ask yourself a two–part question:

1. Does this information need to be sent at all?
2. What is the best way to pass it along?

The first question is the one you have been asking yourself throughout this book. You never confuse quantity with quality. You question whether nice-to-know is worth the effort for the receiver. You make sure the information you send out is good quality.

But what about the second question? When does electronic transmission via e-mail make sense?

Tip: Tap the e-mail experts.

Public-sector employees, including university and government people, are very fortunate to have been the first to have access to e-mail. Many of them are experts at using e-mail in general, and in contacting colleagues all over the world. Think. Whom do you know who works in the public sector? Could they provide valuable tips to you? Ask them.

Here are some guidelines for effective use of e-mail:

1. Send messages that can be answered at the receiver's convenience. Let's face it. Not everyone checks their computer regularly. If your message is time-sensitive, you could miss critical deadlines. *Idea:* Leave a voice mail message saying that an e-mail message is waiting. *Further idea:* Would the phone call alone be sufficient?

2. Contact people in different time zones and countries. Using e-mail is a way to avoid making phone calls at weird hours to colleagues in a different time zone. Also, you can save money. Even if you transmit at expensive daytime phone rates, the elapsed time is so short that the costs are minimal.

3. Send broadcast transmissions to a group of people. If everyone on your committee is linked, then e-mail is great because you don't need to bother creating hard copy at all. What a tool!

4. Convey nonsensitive or nonemotional information. If there are no politically sensitive time bombs contained in your message, e-mail works great. Remember, e-mail is words only. A handwritten fax on letterhead contains a lot of "you." Would that be better in this case? You want to save time, not create situations where more time-consuming explanations will be required.

5. Avoid interrupting people's work. What a powerful use of this tool! What a courtesy to your coworkers! It's very hard for most people to not answer the phone. And answering the phone is disruptive to thought. Sending your message e-mail is a real gift to your receivers because their powers of concentration are undisturbed until they choose to deal with it.

But there are some drawbacks to e-mail use.

Caution number one: E-mail requires typing. This is one more compelling reason to become a crack touch typist. If you're still hunting-and-pecking, use the phone.

Caution number two: E-mail ties up your phone line. If you aren't part of a large system with many phone lines that

Sharing opinions: Are you sharing expertise or venting?

rotate, be aware your phone is sending out a busy signal—you're unavailable to that hot prospect who might be trying to call.

Are you contributing your opinions to electronic chat rooms? If so, ask yourself whether you are venting or sharing expertise.

Venting means you are expressing your opinions with feeling. You don't plan to do anything; you're mostly letting off steam and frustration. For example, "Proposal X is a great idea!" "It's time to begin _____." "Something isn't right about _____." "So-and-so should be stopped from _____."

Everybody needs to vent sometimes. But if you catch yourself spending so much time venting that you sound like a broken record, perhaps it's time to convert your energy into action. Or direct your energy back to one of your focus areas.

Expertise means you have solid credentials in an area and information to share that would not be readily available to the reader. For example, you contribute things like "A source we can use is _____." "Some side effects are _____." "Be careful of _____."

It is very rewarding to help people who are searching for information. Your contribution can be enormous. But if you find large amounts of your time being eaten up, stop yourself. Refocus your energy on your areas of concentration.

Balance is the key. Sharing is an enriching part of life. But so is getting your work done, and that's where your paycheck comes from.

As you finish this book, reflect on all you have accomplished. You no longer (well, rarely) miss deadlines, lose confidential folders, or have to stall your boss for a report. You have credibility as an expert in your important job areas. You sleep better because an entire level of anxiety has been lowered. You are ready for new challenges.

You can't know it all. But you can know all that you need to. And you do!

CONGRATULATIONS AND GRADUATION CEREMONY

Good for you! You are a Graduate Information Master.

You have acquired a valuable skill, the ability to process information, that will enable you to succeed more easily at anything you attempt. Listen to how you sound in staff meetings. Hear that confidence in your voice? Notice how your written materials have become more succinct, focusing on the essential. Doesn't your workspace look nice and orderly? Not necessarily perfect, but certainly functional. It's time to move on.

Celebrate your success. (No one else will do it for you!) Post your Information Master Certificate on your wall. Use it to remind yourself of what you have accomplished, to refresh your memory on the principles, and to stay disciplined when you look longingly at something that is merely nice to know.

Information Master Certificate of Achievement

As a Graduate Information Master who has overcome information overload I accept that:

- I cannot know it all.
- I can know what I need to.

I am committed to:

- Concentrating 80 percent of my effort on information related to my three job focuses, for those are my responsibilities.
- Overcoming weaknesses by using information for my self-improvement area.
- Preparing for tomorrow using information for my future-development area.
- Controlling the flow of both incoming and outgoing information.

I welcome new information, for it is the key to continuous improvement.

Signed: _____ Date: _____

NOTES

NOTES

NOTES

NOTES

NOTES

NOTES